PERSONAL MARRIAGE CONTRACT

John F. Whitaker

PERSONAL MARRIAGE CONTRACT

by
John F. Whitaker, M.D.

 OK Street, Inc.
Dallas, Texas™ 1976

Library of Congress Card Catalog Number: 76-009623

ISBN: 0-917278-00-3

Printed by Taylor Publishing Company, Dallas, Texas

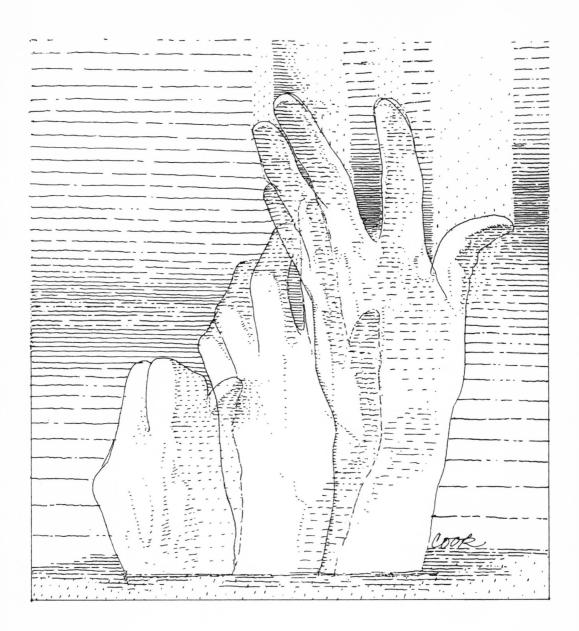

LIVE ON OK STREET

OK STREET is where winners live.

OK STREET is a way of living with the wisdom that living is more than just being alive.

OK STREET winners are enlightened people who are healthy, sincere, brave, assertive, attractive, ambitious, rich, kind, free, fun and loving.

OK STREET winners risk and learn from mistakes, own their time, please themselves with concern and caring for others, are humanly weak at times and are number one because they do it easy.

OK STREET is lined with houses of knowledge where people owning their power are in charge of their destinies and aspire to higher levels of human awareness, development and excellence.

OK STREET neighbors know I am OK and you are OK. "I win, you're invited to win." And since OK STREET is infinite, there is always room for other welcomed people to live, laugh, love, work and win together.

OK STREET winners say no to Not OKness. They are adventuresome people filled with joy who dare to dream, think, work and make their dreams come true. They say: "I know what I want. I deserve it. I can do it. I will do it. WOW!"

ACKNOWLEDGMENTS

My deepest gratitude is extended to the patients in my private practice of psychiatry who asked for and inspired this publication. They decided on the contents by offering crucial feedback about what was and what was not valuable at a practical level in attaining a fulfilling marriage. The sample personal marriage contract has been used successfully by many couples at the time of this publication.

I am especially grateful to John J. O'Hearne, M.D., internationally prominent psychiatrist from Kansas City, Missouri, who reviewed the manuscript and contributed to its final form. Taibi Kahler, Ph.D., clinical psychologist, authority on Transactional Analysis and a special friend, critiqued the manuscript for technical accuracy and provided valuable ideas for improving it. Edward J. Rydman, Ph.D., clinical psychologist and former Executive Director of the American Association of Marriage and Family Counselors, also critiqued the manuscript for technical accuracy and contributed to its final content. Melvyn A. Berke, Ph.D., clinical psychologist and columnist, reviewed the manuscript and offered important suggestions and support. Very special thanks to the following persons for their constructive criticism, advice and review of the manuscript: Raymond H. Abrams, M.D., obstetrician and gynecologist; the Reverend J. Robert Maceo, Jr., Episcopal minister; and Fayteen Holman, M.Ed., counselor.

I also wish to acknowledge the invaluable consultation of Peter Wolf of Peter Wolf Associates, Inc. Prominent author and journalist, Dudley Lynch, offered critical appraisal and encouragement as he edited the manuscript for publication. Thanks to John Cook for the warm and tender illustrations. I am profoundly grateful to Walter B. Hailey, Jr. and Jerry W. Peeples for their encouragement, friendship and administrative consultation. Finally, for providing inspiration, ideas and supervising the production of the publication, I am deeply thankful to Judy Bergen.

CONTENTS

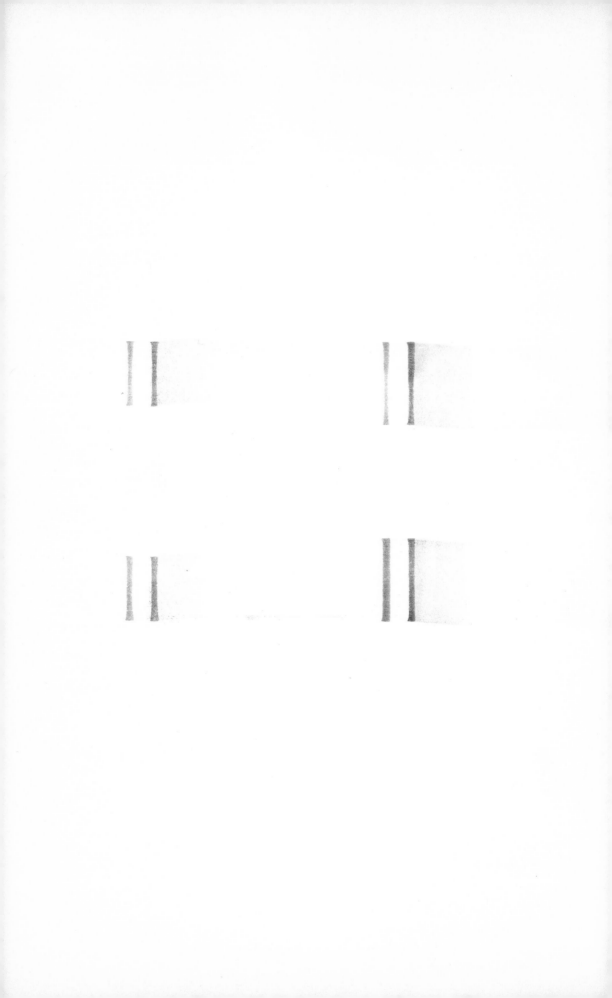

PERSONAL MARRIAGE CONTRACT

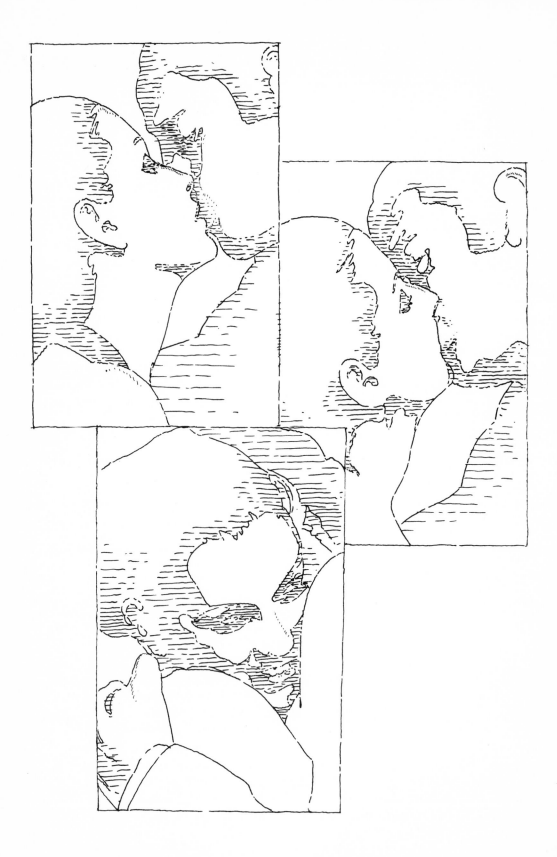

A BRAVE NEW RELATIONSHIP

Marital or relationship difficulties are the most common reasons why people seek out my private practice of psychiatry for psychotherapy and counseling. Couples are more experimental and creative in their design of life styles and relationships than ever before. The advent of increased freedom and societal permissiveness brings a challenging responsibility to individuals who are willing to enter the most exciting adventure of all: continuing love with another human being.

With new permissions from society to leave a relationship that is not exciting and satisfying, the challenge to each couple is to create a marriage in which both will *want to* stay rather than be obligated to stay. No matter how damaged a relationship is, when both partners are willing, there is reason for realistic HOPE. Any relationship can be converted to one which is filled with satisfying creative work, fun, consistent romance, freedom for individual and mutual fulfillment, love and security. For accomplishing this, an effective tool which is growing rapidly in popularity is the *personal marriage contract*.

The personal marriage contract can be used by singles to clarify their view on marriage and ongoing friendships. It can be used by couples considering or planning a marriage. The contract has proven helpful to already happily married individuals who ambitiously aspire to higher levels of fulfillment in their marriages. It has been found useful by people about to divorce or already divorced. It has been a remarkably useful instrument for resolving the problems of a relationship in trouble.

There are three types of marriage contracts: the legal, the religious and the personal. It is not within the province of this writing to deal with the legal or religious. Readers are referred to attorneys-at-law or the clergy for counsel in these areas. Also, this personal contract is not to replace the formal wedding ceremony. Many couples are now adding more depth, meaning and lasting significance to their formal wedding ceremony by creatively working together to design their own public celebration.

The personal marriage contract is a writing made by the parties involved to evidence the terms and conditions of their commitments. Consequently, each party knows what to count on and expect from the other. With fulfillment of the defined promises, trust results, and ongoing love is possible. This is a means of making expectations explicit and open, rather than implied and vague.

The sample personal marriage contract presented in this text may be accepted as it is. However, couples are encouraged to personalize it by appropriate negotiated modifications, deletions or additions. A good contract should be broad enough to permit a sense of freedom and restrictive enough to offer security. Some couples add guidelines about responsibility for birth control, division of responsibility in handling household chores and payment of bills.

The contract is not meant to be read, signed and put away. Couples are encouraged to read and reread their contracts separately and together — refresh, review, renew, revive, reinforce and reexperience. The contract is to be used as a working and inspiring part of the relationship. As the relationship grows and changes, so will the depth and meaning of the contract grow and change.

With relationships in trouble, it is recommended that the couple seek help from a competent professional and invest a period of one year before considering the alternative of divorce. It is not recommended that the couple live separately during this time. During the year each partner has an opportunity to grow separately as an individual and an opportunity to grow together as a couple. The worst that can happen is that each will grow in relationship skills which will be an advantage whether the couple stays together in an OK marriage or proceeds with an OK divorce.

Love is more than a feeling. Love means action and requires skill. "I love hearing you say that you love me, but more important, show me." The ten major Skill-Action areas of love are outlined in the next section.

This book is dedicated to those people who wish to live on OK STREET in a committed relationship filled with both practical security and romantic excitement.

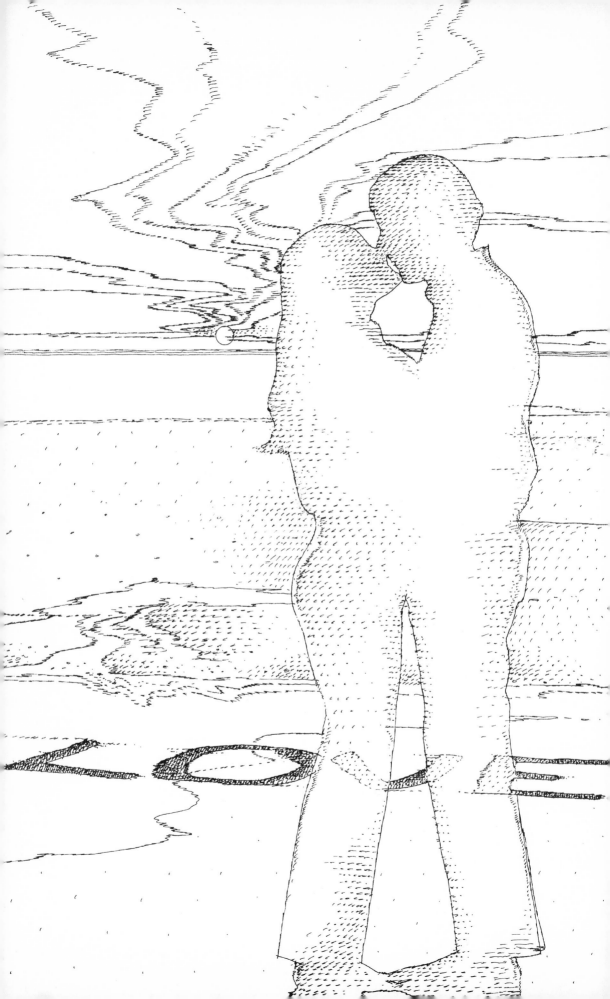

ACTS OF LOVE

Frequently, my patients with relationship problems ask, "What is love, and how do I show love?" Some realize for the first time that they have never really known.

The definition of marital love is subjective and will vary, reflecting the uniqueness of each individual. However, in my work with couples through the years, I have noted that those who regard their marriages as successful have developed awareness, skill and action in ten key areas.

Ten SKILL-ACTION Areas of Loving:

1. Withness	6. Nurturing
2. Friends	7. Strokes
3. Work	8. Sex
4. Rights	9. Quarrels
5. Time	10. Contract

WITHNESS

Love is wanting to be with you.

Develop an attitude and behavior that reflects wanting to belong *with,* not having to belong *to.* Be together, but yet be separate. Want, not desperately need. Be with and involved, but not possessed or possessive. Be aware that you own yourself and that another cannot own you. You can be close *and* free. Love means *want to* not *have to.* Avoid over-dependence — "I can't live without you," signed, Desperate. Avoid under-dependence — "I don't need anybody," signed, Belligerent. Experience inter-dependence — "I enjoy being me and being with you," signed, Warm.

FRIENDS

Love is not limiting or exclusive.

Don't count on only one person to fulfill all your wants and needs. This fosters over-dependence, which breeds hostility. Have at least three real friends outside the marriage who can be counted on for communication and fun, and who will want to be there to help at bad times. Be aware of the difference between real friends and acquaintances. Outside friendships protect against marital symbiosis, which destroys love. Next to yourself, your marital partner can be your very best friend. However, your marital partner cannot be your only friend.

WORK

Love is enjoying work together.

Learn effective communication techniques for solving the inevitable problems which must be dealt with in a relationship. Openly communicate feelings and ideas — and know the difference. Love is knowing and being known. Be solution oriented rather than problem oriented. State the problem clearly, review the solution options, discuss advantages and disadvantages of the options and then reach a mutually acceptable solution. If an impasse is reached, schedule another specific time for work on the problem. Work is not something you have to do and play something you want to do. Play while you work so that work together is exciting. Take charge of problems instead of waiting for them to work themselves out. It may be a long, long wait. Love, like fire, once sparked, is sustained by working together.

RIGHTS

Love is respecting my rights and yours.

Define areas of rights, privileges and responsibilities. Individuals maintain their OKness by asserting power to nourish and protect their rights. When the people within a marriage are OK then the marriage is OK. Some of the most exciting aspects of new marriages are the possibilities resulting from the emergence of sexual equality. Have a partner instead of a master or a slave. Assert your right to your own time, space, money, friends, work and privacy. Respect these same rights of your partner.

TIME

Love is sharing our time, our life, our nows.

At birth each individual is given a finite wealth of time to spend and invest. There are no deposits, only withdrawals. Time can be spent with wisdom and planning or it can be squandered away with ignorance and recklessness. Life is valuable, so time is precious. Ask yourself these questions: Why am I here? What am I doing here and now with my time? Own your time, don't be pushed or controlled by it. When you are rushing you are not loving. Actively structure time in the relationship so that there is interesting rhythm and contrast. Avoid waiting passively for "things to happen". Love means staying in the NOW while planning for future NOWS. Structure time separately and together. Consistently plan time for aloneness, work, communication and fun. Individuals tend to contrive conflict and anger to relieve boredom when there is not stimulation from winning and fun. Remember fun! Without fun the marriage may be dead, boring and frustrating. Make out a fun list of at least 100 ways you like to have fun and share it with your partner. Don't nag or push someone to have fun. If you want more fun and romance, be fun, romantic and exciting first as an invitation to join you. Structure time primarily around wins instead of awfuls. Remember to plan unplanned time for impulsiveness and spontaneity. Love is not being restricted by time.

NURTURING

Love is tenderly caring for me and you at times of need.

When you are committed to OKness from within, you are not emotionally vulnerable to anyone. Love is not a fearful risk. Love is a joy. Nurturing means counting on yourself to maintain your OKness no matter what. By trusting yourself to care for you first, you are then in a position to trust and offer the same care to others. Whereas you are not responsible for making the partner feel good, you are responsible to yourself to experience the joy of inviting your partner to accept acts of nurturing. When loving care is given to another you are simultaneously giving joy to yourself. Nurturing is being to yourself and your partner: caring, concerned, compassionate, empathetic, considerate, kind, forgiving, reassuring, understanding, reasonably permissive, nonjudgmental, sympathetic, listening, warmly stroking and encouraging. Nurturing means being there at the bad times as well as the good. Nurturing means not attempting to stifle the other's fun. With the security of predictable nurturing, "I will be me and you can be you, without fear."

STROKES

*Love is giving, asking, taking, saying "no",
cooing and wowing.*

A key act of love is the recognition, or
strokes, one partner shares with the other. Love
means not just feeling, but saying and showing,
"I love you." Consistently give good positive
strokes, even though the partner has heard them
before. Strokes are like food; you need them
every day. Give positive strokes for qualities and
behavior that you like. What you stroke is what
you get. Say what you don't like without
attacking. When positive strokes are offered,
accept them with enthusiastic responsiveness.
Ask for the strokes you want clearly and with
assertiveness. To ask for strokes does not
diminish their value. Avoid TGF (taken for
granted). Be certain you get your MDR
(minimum daily requirement) of touching . . .
hand holding, warm hugs, body massages. Say
"no" to what you don't want without belligerence
and with consideration for the other. Refuse to
accept strokes that you don't want, like put
downs. Learn to ignore negatives that are
offered or say something like, "Go suck a pickle!"

SEX

Love is experiencing ultimate joy in our sexual union.

Love means the willing act of giving, taking and sharing yourself in the act of sexual intercourse. Sex in the context of love has been described as the most intense and ultimate human experience. Sex is for fun, and sharing fun is loving. Protect this important area by planning time for love in a good environment. Know the difference between nurturing and sexual needs. Restore yourself by having nurturing needs met prior to sex. Avoid overworking, overeating or overdrinking alcoholic beverages. Keep your body clean, physically healthy and attractive. Avoid ritualization, monotony and boredom. Anytime, anywhere, anything goes as long as both feel OK. As with all acts of love, stay in the NOW. Keep your mind free of hassle. It is your major sex organ.

QUARRELS

Love is sharing bad feelings as well as good.

When you are frustrated or mad, you are not caring and loving. Because of the importance of clearing away the inevitable trash that is generated in a marriage, most couples make contracts to facilitate constructive quarreling. A good or constructive quarrel is one in which everyone wins. Significant growth in relationships often results. Understand that in your humanness you may experience frustration when you have wishes that are not carried to fulfillment. If frustrations are not expressed and resolved, you will tend to resurrect vivid vengeful memories that will cut off your joy. Paradoxically, when effective quarreling techniques are practiced, not much time is spent in anger. Discuss and then mutually accept guidelines for quarreling. Be aware of when you are feeling frustration. Don't withdraw and simmer, confront and resolve.

Dearest Pete,
My lifelong friend.
I love you today
Susie

CONTRACT

Love is trusting me and you.

Although love may exist in brief encounters, most people seek long term relationships with historical depth, predictability and security — a satisfaction of growing older together. Your marriage does not give you security. You give yourself security from within by knowing that you will count on yourself no matter what. You may choose to enhance the quality of your security by your mutual trustworthiness in your marriage. Commitments in a marriage require more than sexual fidelity and promises of good intentions to make a marriage work. A specific, encompassing personal marriage contract should be mutually designed. Decide what you want. You deserve to have your dreams come true. Decide that you can do it. Then do it. Enjoy the results. What you feel toward others and do with others is a projection of what you are already feeling and doing with yourself. Love and trust of others begins by loving and trusting yourself. When you promise yourself something, be reliable. Do it! Be assertive to invite others to keep the spirit and literal interpretation of their promises. See the suggested sample personal marriage contract presented in this text.

SAMPLE

PERSONAL MARRIAGE CONTRACT

Declaration of Commitment

This contract is a jointly owned plan by

_____

and

_____

which is to begin on the _____ day of

_____ A.D. _____, extend

for a period of (2, 3, 4, 5 or more) _____

years (or indefinite) and terminate on

the _____ day of _____ A.D. ____

(or indefinite). On the date of termination,

we will reconfirm or renegotiate the contract;

or we will cease being WITH each other, will

part in a friendly manner and will go on with

our lives separately.

_____
signature

_____
signature

dated _____ A.D. _____

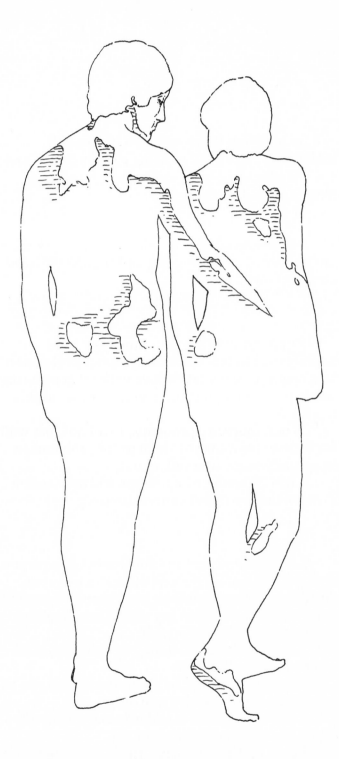

Declaration of Commitment

I am entering this contract with the full understanding of the exciting risks involved and a willingness to give up unrealistic myths, no matter how cherished:

I understand that nothing is forever, there are no absolute guarantees, and that NOW is the only real forever.

I understand that ". . . and they lived happily ever after" exists only in fairy tales, and that sustaining romantic love without continuing work, planning and effective interpersonal skill is a myth.

When there are problems, I will not just wait for time to take care of them or for problems to eventually work themselves out.

I will be aware of problems and take action to solve them without procrastinating.

I understand that my fulfillment as a person does not ultimately depend upon you nor upon any other person, and that, even though I commit to be with you, I accept my ultimate aloneness and responsibility for myself.

I cannot make you happy or unhappy, but I can make myself happy.

My happiness will be an invitation for you to join me in happiness, joy and love.

I will set my own standards and ultimately depend upon myself for approval.

I give up the myth that there is a "one and only" who will make me happy.

Declaration of Commitment

I understand that freedom defined as no commitments or responsibilities is a myth.

When I make commitments to do what I want to do, then I am being free.

Freedom to be me and own myself comes from within — not from you or circumstances around me.

There is no freedom without responsibility.

By being responsible I will be free.

Also, there is no entrapment except as an illusion.

I cannot own another human being nor can I be owned as a possession of another.

Our contract is good only if we achieve maximum individual freedom with the security of predictability.

I understand that there is no absolute equality between standards and characteristics in people who are separate and different; there is equality of rights between people.

I give up the myth that our relationship cannot have different standards.

We are separate people with our own standards and they must never be fused into one standard.

I will feel pride in myself and my differences from you without competing in an "I win, you lose" sense.

I will feel pride in you and your differences from me.

Declaration of Commitment

    I understand that emotional vulnerability is a myth.

    No one can take away my power, which is my capacity to assert myself to achieve my wishes; no one can control me or make me do anything.

    Power defined as the capacity of others to manipulate or influence me to do their bidding against my will is a myth.

    I understand that there will be pain as well as joy, and I accept the risk of a brief period of grief when we part.

    I know that I must ultimately give up everyone I love, unless I die first.

Declaration of Commitment

I will love, honor, respect, but not obey nor subjugate myself to you until either of us changes his mind and maintains a change of attitude for a period of one year or until the termination date of the contract.

I will stay with you during bad times as well as good.

I will be by your side with caring, kindness, compassion, understanding, consideration and warmth during sickness and natural disaster as well as during health and periods free of disaster.

I will not be counted on for caring and compassion at repeated times of contrived illness or disaster.

While I will be strong with you when you feel weak, I expect you likewise to be strong with me when I feel weak.

I will accept you as you are, not attack you nor diminish you publicly nor privately, nor push you to change those things that I do not like about you.

I understand the difference between a role (like husband and wife) and a person. I will not diminish you by thinking of you as "the wife" or "the husband".

I will cherish you as a unique person.

Declaration of Commitment

I will consistently remember those qualities and traits that are beautiful about you and consistently communicate my love by recognizing your inner beauty and your outer physical beauty through words and action.

I will give to you for my inner joy, not from duty, in the NOW without feeling that "I have to" or "you owe me".

I will keep my mind healthy, attractive and loveable.

This will be evinced by my exciting openness to new ideas, my continued education and my acquisition of new skills.

I will expect the same of you and support you fully with my responsiveness and encouragement.

Don't expect me to accept you as you are when you fail to maintain mental attractiveness and fail to take care of your mind.

I will expect you to value your mind.

Declaration of Commitment

I will keep my body healthy, attractive and loveable.

This will be evinced by my grooming, clothing, weight and exercise.

I will expect the same of you and support you fully with my responsiveness and encouragement.

Don't expect me to accept you as you are when you fail to maintain physical attractiveness and fail to take care of your body.

I will expect you to value your body.

I will ask clearly for whatever I wish from you without feeling that I'm begging, without feeling that I shouldn't have to ask and without assuming that you can read my mind.

I will put myself first.

By keeping myself full, satisfied and not hungry, I will have an abundance of joy, love and caring to give to you.

Then, when I give love to you, I am experiencing love for myself.

I will not attempt to control or be controlled by money.

I will own my separate money and property, and enjoy sharing ownership with you of our common money and property.

Since you and I are not children, the concepts of giving and accepting an "allowance", checking up on the other's money spending and asking permission of the other to spend money is not relevant to our relationship.

I will share an equal responsibility with you in understanding and planning our mutual finances.

Declaration of Commitment

Whenever we are confronted with a problem, I will resolve my feelings first, and then, with a cool mind, rationally solve any mutual problems with you.

I will never consider ending any of our commitments while angry or upset.

I understand that you and I in our humanness will make mistakes.

I will not expect either of us to be perfect.

I will accept you as good enough without being 100% in everything.

I will declare those matters of such importance that I do require 100% for my love to continue.

I will be reliable so that we will maintain a basis for trust between us.

I won't say that I will do anything unless I truly want to and unless I actually will.

While I accept the right to have private areas of my life that I will not share with you, I will not sneak on you, nor will I lie to you by either active commission or by failure to share relevant information that affects our relationship.

I will not give come-on signals to others for sexual relations when I see you feel threatened.

I will count on you to recognize, admire and stroke me for my sexuality and attractiveness as a man or woman.

I will respond with genuine reassurance when you feel fears of abandonment.

Declaration of Commitment

I will respect, accept and appreciate your saying NO.

I understand that only by our mutual acceptance of NO will we both be able to say YES and mean it fully.

Furthermore, I understand that by our acceptance of NO we enhance each other's capacity to more fully experience our individuality and separateness within our relationship.

While I accept our momentary human response of frustration with disappointment, I will not act rejected, will not sulk nor continue to be hurt or angry; nor will I attempt to control your expression of your individuality in any way.

I will accept your bad feelings of anger, sadness, helplessness and fear as well as joy.

I will listen to your expressions of frustration without taking your feelings as a personal attack and without trying to control your expressions of feeling in any way.

I will have good quarrels in which we both win whenever I experience bad feelings that may interfere with our closeness and love.

I will not harbor grudges nor keep vengeful feelings.

When I feel bad, I will come to you face to face with my feelings.

No matter how angry or upset I get, I will never threaten to nor actually harm you physically; I will never threaten to nor actually harm myself; I will never threaten to nor actually abandon you, "drop out" or "go crazy".

I will keep my commitments set forth in our contract on quarreling, and provide every opportunity for us both to win in our quarrels.

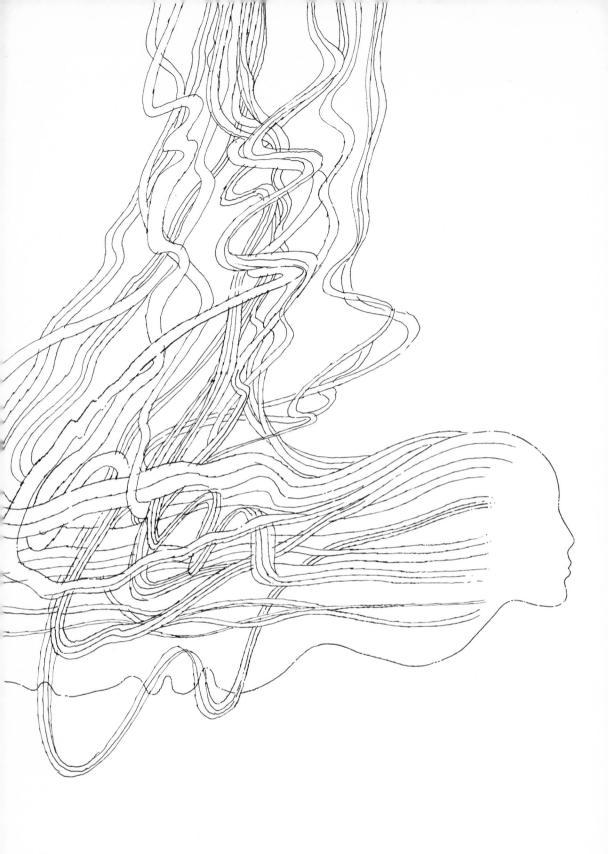

Declaration of Commitment

While I will not accept responsibility for your feelings or behavior, I will accept my responsibility to myself for whatever I do with you.

I understand that in your love you have exposed your human weaknesses.

I will respond to you with reasonable consideration to cherish and invite you to feel protection from undue pain.

I will never ridicule, tease you or use vengefully what you have trusted me to know about you.

I will leave the past behind.

I will henceforth resolve all bad feelings about either of our past mistakes and never bring them up to you.

I understand that being sorry for my past mistakes does not help you or me now, so I will give up any sorrow that I feel for past mistakes.

I will give up wishing that anything in the past was different because, no matter how much I wish, my wishing will not change it now.

While I will learn from the past, I will not live in it.

I will experience being with you NOW while sharing hopes, dreams and plans for the future.

Declaration of Commitment

Since I understand that we cannot be everything to each other, I will respect and value the importance of your having separate play and work activities with separate friends and co-workers.

There are limits with which I will not feel OK.

I will be aware of my limits of acceptance and let you know clearly.

I will respect your confidences and never share with another those things that you share with me privately without obtaining your agreement in advance.

I will keep this commitment even should we part.

I will place high priority and value on our fun together.

I understand that for us to want to stay together and be free of boredom, we must share enthusiasm and responsiveness.

So, I will consistently enjoy sharing those parts of myself which you enjoy.

While I accept my right to withdrawal time and separateness within our relationship and our home, I will not unexpectedly switch on you and withdraw following an explicit or implied promise to share myself with you.

I will not take you for granted.

Declaration of Commitment

I will value and protect our sexual expression of sharing fun and love.

I will not use sex ulteriorly to express anything but love.

I will experience closeness and love with you as a person prior to sexual union.

I will place high value on our sexual love, and will be open to you sexually.

At times I may not wish to be open.

Then I will not pick a fight, but I will tell you clearly with kindness and consideration. I will have warm feelings with the knowledge that I am loved and wanted.

I will make time consistently available for BEING together for communication, work, fun and love.

No matter how many demands or enticements I experience for "success" or child-raising, I will give OUR time the highest priority.

Although my work and our children are important, you are more important; and what I give to myself WITH you is more important.

Declaration of Commitment

I will place the highest priority on my loyalty to you above outside work or commitments to any organizations.

No matter what demands or enticements confront me, monetary or otherwise, I will not change our location or residence without considering your feelings and ideas and without your full agreement.

Don't count on me just to follow you wherever you go.

I will share in the parenting experience of providing care, authority and opportunity for our little ones to grow and achieve their own wishes, hopes and dreams.

While I will at times of need, give higher priority to our children, overall, I will give the highest priority to our relationship.

Or: (I will leave the question of future children open, and I will discuss and consider your feelings and ideas prior to making a mutually planned decision about children.)